Bugs

Hercules Beetles

by Trudy Becker

FOCUS READERS®

PIONEER

www.focusreaders.com

Focus Readers is distributed by North Star Editions:
sales@northstareditions.com | 888-417-0195

Produced for Focus Readers by Red Line Editorial.

Photographs ©: Shutterstock Images, cover, 1, 6, 10, 12, 14, 17, 20; Gilles Martin/Gamma-Rapho/Getty Images, 4; iStockphoto, 8; Steve Taylor ARPS/Alamy, 18

Library of Congress Cataloging-in-Publication Data
Names: Becker, Trudy, author.
Title: Hercules beetles / by Trudy Becker.
Description: Lake Elmo, MN : Focus Readers, [2023] | Series: Bugs |
   Includes index. | Audience: Grades 2-3
Identifiers: LCCN 2022033360 (print) | LCCN 2022033361 (ebook) | ISBN
   9781637394519 (hardcover) | ISBN 9781637394885 (paperback) | ISBN
   9781637395615 (pdf) | ISBN 9781637395257 (ebook)
Subjects: LCSH: Hercules beetle--Juvenile literature.
Classification: LCC QL596.S3 B43 2023 (print) | LCC QL596.S3 (ebook) |
   DDC 595.76--dc23/eng/20220726
LC record available at https://lccn.loc.gov/2022033360
LC ebook record available at https://lccn.loc.gov/2022033361

Printed in the United States of America
Mankato, MN
012023

About the Author

Trudy Becker lives in Minneapolis, Minnesota. She likes exploring new places and loves anything involving books.

Table of Contents

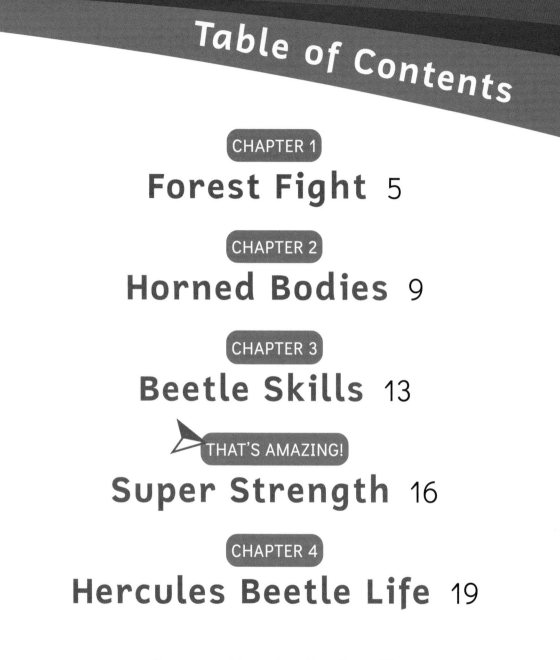

Chapter 1

Forest Fight

Two Hercules beetles fight on the forest floor. Their huge horns crash together. One beetle lifts the other up. He smashes his enemy to the ground. He won the fight.

Hercules beetles live in rainforests. They are found in Central and South America. They stay hidden during the day. But at night, they come out. They crawl through the forest.

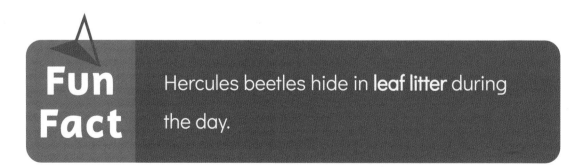

Fun Fact

Hercules beetles hide in **leaf litter** during the day.

Chapter 2

Horned Bodies

Hercules beetles are longer than most beetles. One can be as long as an adult's hand. Each beetle has six legs. It has two sets of wings. It also has a tough **exoskeleton**.

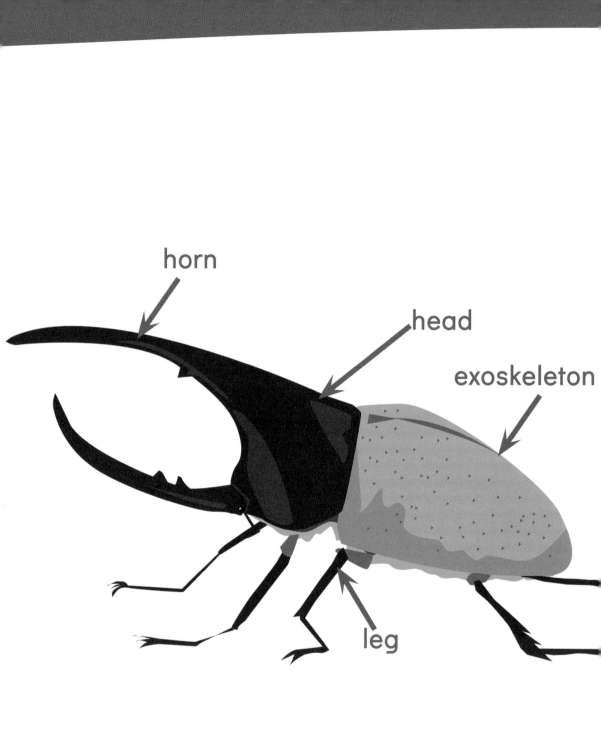

Male Hercules beetles have huge horns. The bottom horn can be short. But the top horn is long and strong. Males use their horns to fight or dig.

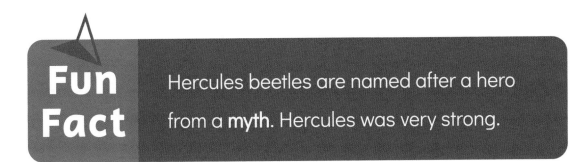

Fun Fact

Hercules beetles are named after a hero from a **myth**. Hercules was very strong.

Chapter 3

Beetle Skills

Hercules beetles have many **predators**. Some birds eat them. Rats eat them, too. So, the beetles hiss or put out a bad smell. That keeps predators away.

Sometimes Hercules beetles change colors. Their exoskeletons can look black, green, or yellow. **Scientists** aren't sure why. It might help the beetles hide at night.

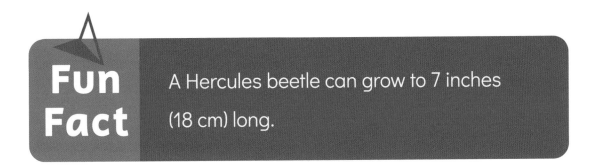

Fun Fact

A Hercules beetle can grow to 7 inches (18 cm) long.

Super Strength

Hercules beetles are very strong. They can lift 850 times their own weight. That's like a person lifting six school buses. Male beetles use their super strength in fights. The winner gets to **mate** with a female.

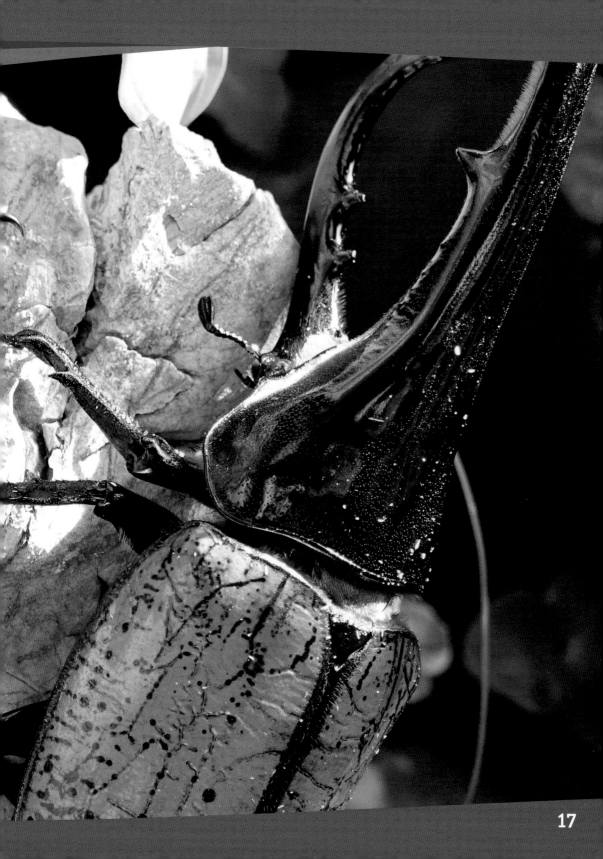

Chapter 4

Hercules Beetle Life

Hercules beetles spend most of their time eating. They are **herbivores**. Young Hercules beetles eat rotten wood. Adult beetles eat fruit.

Female Hercules beetles lay eggs in the ground or in dead wood. The eggs hatch after a month. The baby beetles stay underground. That is where they grow into adults. Then they come up to the surface.

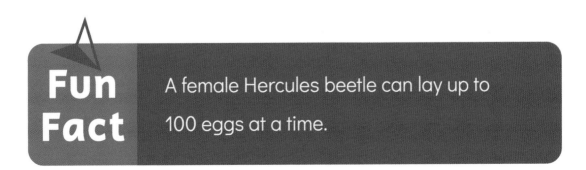

Fun Fact

A female Hercules beetle can lay up to 100 eggs at a time.

FOCUS ON
Hercules Beetles

Write your answers on a separate piece of paper.

1. Write a sentence that explains the main idea of Chapter 4.

2. Do you think it would be helpful for humans to have horns like Hercules beetles? Why or why not?

3. Where do Hercules beetles hide during the day?
   - A. on tree trunks
   - B. in leaf litter
   - C. under birds' nests

4. Why is an exoskeleton useful?
   - A. It protects the body.
   - B. It is shiny and pretty.
   - C. It scares away predators.

Answer key on page 24.

Glossary

exoskeleton
A hard shell that protects an animal's body.

herbivores
Animals that eat mostly plants.

leaf litter
Dead or rotting plant material on the ground.

mate
To come together to make a baby.

myth
A well-known, fictional story common to a group of people.

predators
Animals that hunt other animals for food.

scientists
People who study things to learn how they work.

To Learn More

BOOKS

Garstecki, Julia. *Fast Facts About Beetles*. North Mankato, MN: Capstone Press, 2021.

Hansen, Grace. *Hercules Beetle*. Minneapolis: Abdo Publishing, 2022.

NOTE TO EDUCATORS

Visit **www.focusreaders.com** to find lesson plans, activities, links, and other resources related to this title.

Index

Answer Key: 1. Answers will vary; **2.** Answers will vary; **3.** B; **4.** A